Baby photo

My Parents

My earliest memories of my mum and dad

What I remember most about my parents

Important lessons they taught me

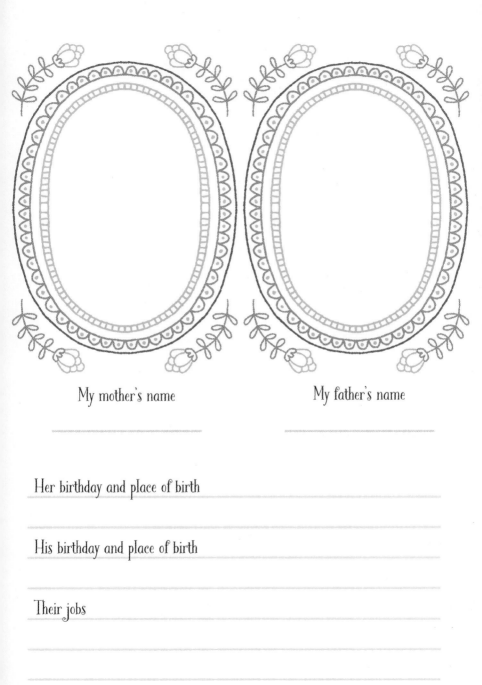

My mother's name

My father's name

Her birthday and place of birth

His birthday and place of birth

Their jobs

How my parents met

_____

_____

When and where they were married

_____

_____

GRANDMA REMEMBERS

A JOURNAL TO COMPLETE
WITH TREASURED MEMORIES

COMPILED BY KAREN DOLBY

Michael O'Mara Books Limited

My Story Begins

The day and place I was born

The time of my birth

I weighed

My full name

Those names were chosen because ...

My favourite story about my mother

My favourite story about my father

My Grandparents

My father's parents

Names	Dates of birth	Places of birth

Where they lived

Their occupations

Stories I know about them

 My mother's parents

Names	Dates of birth	Places of birth

Where they lived

Their occupations

Stories I know about them

Our Family History

My favourite family photo

Family stories that were passed down to me

Family Photos

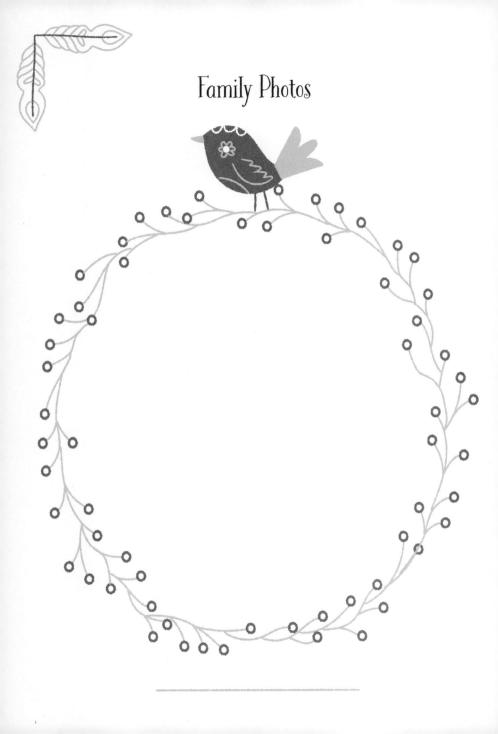

My Brothers and Sisters

My brothers' and sisters' names

The dates and places they were born

The brother or sister I was closest to growing up

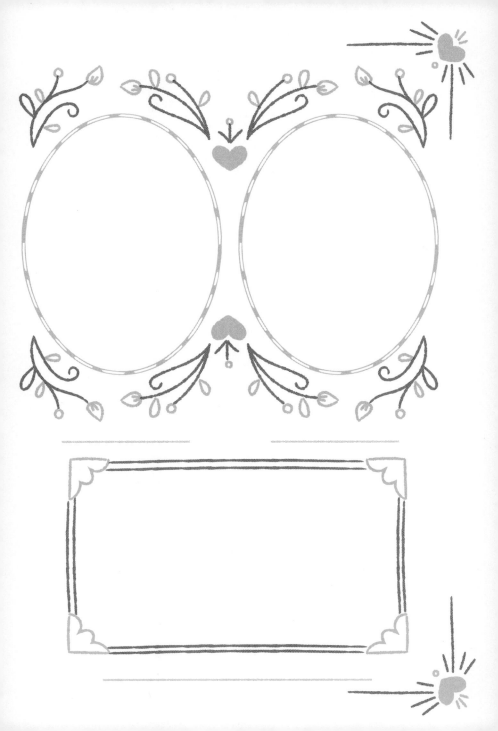

Sibling Stories

Stories about my sisters and brothers

What they went on to do as adults

Where they live now

Their families

Cousins

My cousins' names

Times we spent together as children

My favourite cousin

Sometimes we squabbled

My best memory of my cousins

Where they are now

When I Was Young

The first thing I can remember

Stories from my childhood

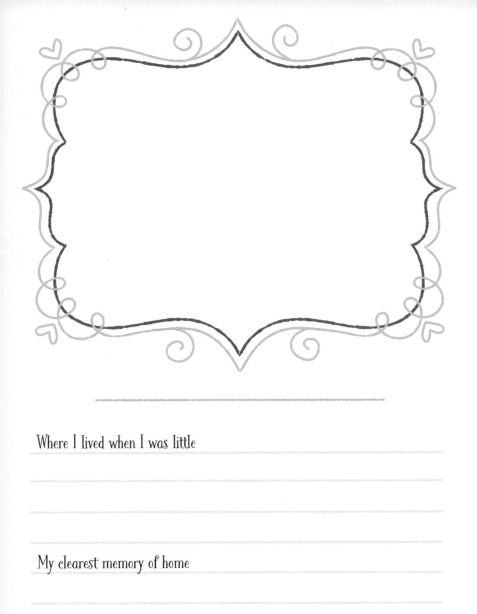

Where I lived when I was little

My clearest memory of home

Growing Up

My first memory

When I grew up I
wanted to be ...

My favourite toy

The games we played

My best friends' names

Family rules

Pocket money I was given and
what I usually spent it on

Childhood Pets

Family pets

My first pet

_____

Stories about our pets

At Home

Memorable family get-togethers from my childhood

_____

_____

_____

_____

_____

At Christmas my family would always ...

_____

_____

_____

_____

_____

Birthday celebrations

_____

_____

_____

My favourite meals

My least favourite food

School Days

What I remember about my first day

_____

_____

_____

_____

_____

_____

_____

_____

_____

_____

_____

_____

_____

_____

_____

_____

School photo

My favourite teacher was ...

My least favourite teacher was ...

Rules and regulations

My favourite subjects

My least favourite subjects

Learning a musical instrument

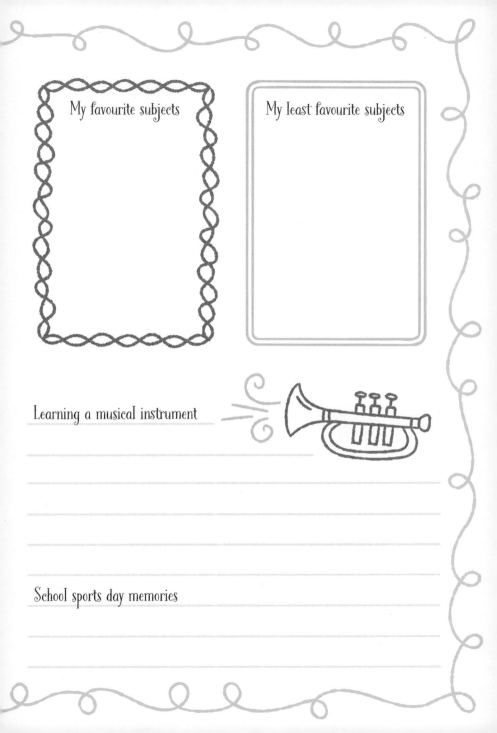

School sports day memories

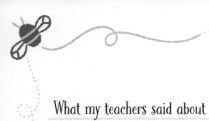

What my teachers said about me

My best friends

Stories from my school days

My age when I left school

My exam results

As a Teenager, These Were a Few of My Favourite Things

Colour

Book

Game

Singer or group

Song

Film

Actor

Sport

Season

Flower

Food

Holiday

When I was young I wanted to be ...

Young and Carefree

As a teenager I used to ...

Ways in which life was different from today when I was growing up

Where we socialized

My best friends

Me as a teenager

What we wore

The craziest fashions from my youth

My first boyfriend

On Leaving School

Following on from school I ...

I wanted to be ...

Memories from this time

For the Record

My height

My build

My shoe size

The colour of my eyes

My natural hair colour

I am blood group

My distinguishing features

My best feature

If I could change one thing about me it would be ...

My Working Life

My first full-time job

_____

_____

What I earned

_____

_____

People I worked with

_____

The hours I worked

_____

_____

Travel to and from work

_____

All Work and No Play

My next job

Other places I worked

My ambitions

More colleagues

Where I lived

Socializing and Friends

It was not all hard work. In my free time I liked to ...

_____

_____

_____

Friends I socialized with

_____

_____

_____

Where we used to go

_____

_____

_____

Things I enjoyed doing

_____

_____

_____

As I Grew Up, These Were a Few More of My Favourite Things

Pastime or hobby

Book

Film

Actor

Song

Singer

Outfit

Place

Evening out

My biggest ambition at the time

If I could give my younger self one piece of advice it would be ...

Meeting Your Grandfather

The first words he said to me

Where we met

Where he worked

Things we liked to do

When and where he proposed

Our first date

My first impression of him

His first impression of me

Our Wedding

The time and date

The wedding service took place at ...

The reception was held at ...

The wedding meal

What I wore

In the bridal bouquet

The ring

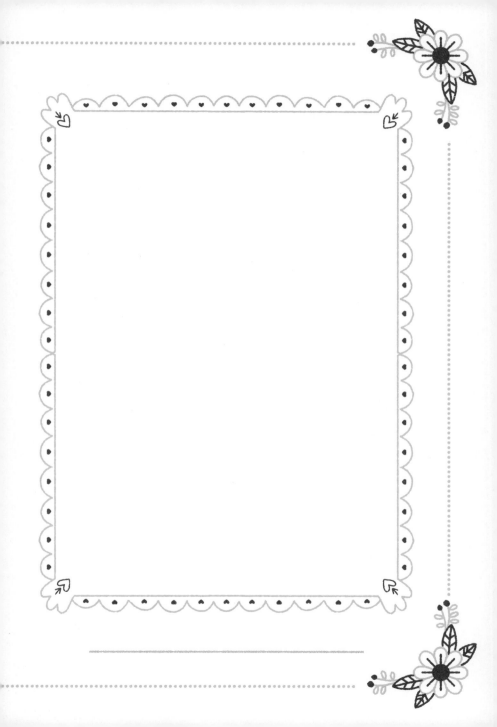

At the Wedding

My bridesmaids

The best man

On the guest list

Our first dance was to

My favourite memory of the day

The Honeymoon

We honeymooned in ...

_____

_____

_____

_____

_____

Where we stayed

_____

_____

_____

A funny thing happened ...

_____

_____

_____

Your Grandfather's Family

Your grandfather's father's name was

Your grandfather's mother's name was

His brothers' and sisters' names were

Where they lived

My favourite stories about my in-laws

Our First Home

Where we lived when we were first married

Moving in

How long we stayed there

Choosing furniture and china

What I remember most about our first home

Places I Have Lived

Moving on from our first home

Where we went next

My other homes

My favourite place to live

Memories I cherish of the places I've lived

Food for Two

How I learned to cook

_____

_____

_____

_____

The first meal I ever made

_____

_____

_____

_____

When it all went wrong

_____

_____

_____

_____

Our favourite food

Memorable meals we ate

The Birth of My Children

Full name	Why we chose that name	Date and place of birth

Weight	Eye colour	Hair colour

Children do the Funniest things

Funny stories from when my children were small that still make me laugh

First words and funny phrases

Strange habits

Embarrassing moments

Family Life

When our children were young, this is what a typical day was like

_____

_____

_____

School stories

_____

_____

At weekends we often ...

_____

_____

A few special memories from this time

_____

_____

_____

_____

Family Moments

Our first family pet

Other pets

My children's hobbies

Things that made
me proud

Household rules and duties

As teenagers, my children's favourite
music was ...

Sports we all played

Family Occasions

How we celebrated birthdays

_____

_____

_____

Our family Christmas traditions

_____

_____

_____

_____

_____

Other family traditions

_____

_____

_____

The special occasions I remember best

Favourite Family Recipes

Here are a few old family favourites that have been
made again and again over the years

Recipe

Recipe

Recipe

Recipe

Your Mum or Dad

What your mum or dad was like as a child

... and as a teenager

My favourite memory of them

Your Parents

How your parents met

Meeting my new son- or daughter-in-law

My first impressions

Have you heard the story?

Grandchildren

My first grandchild's name and date of birth

My grandchildren so far

Full name | Date and place of birth

Some stories about my grandchildren

You

When you were born

How I heard the news

When I first saw you

I thought you looked like ...

My favourite memories of you

When We're All Together

Of all the family times we've spent together these are some of the most memorable

_____

_____

The best outing

_____

_____

This still makes me laugh

_____

_____

_____

_____

The most embarrassing

_____

_____

My favourite memory

Memorable family parties

What makes us special

Advice to Grandchildren

I'm very proud of my grandchildren and when I'm boasting
about you all, this is what I say

The advice I would give my grandchildren

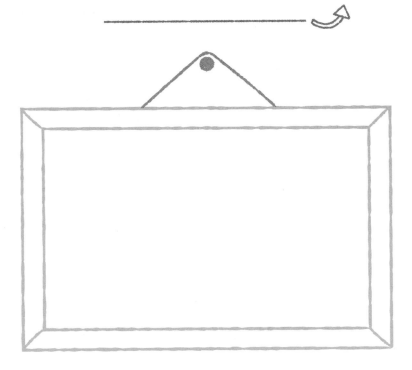

As a Grandmother, These are More of My Favourite Things

Season
_____

Day
_____

Month
_____

Flower
_____

Colour
_____

Scent
_____

The perfume I wear
_____

Jewel

Place

Book

Drink

Food

Treat

Hobby

My Desert Island Records

1.

2.

3.

4.

5.

6.

7.

8.

Why I've chosen these eight pieces of music

And if all but one were lost, I would keep ...

Because ...

My Top Ten Films

1.

2.

3.

4.

5.

6.

7.

8.

9.

10.

What makes these films special to me

Hobbies

My favourite ways to spend my spare time

_____

_____

_____

_____

_____

_____

Other passions over the years

_____

_____

_____

_____

_____

_____

Things I've Learned and Tips I'd Like to Pass On

My Best and Oldest Friends

My best friends during my life

_____

_____

_____

_____

How we met

_____

_____

_____

_____

What has made them so important to me

_____

_____

_____

_____

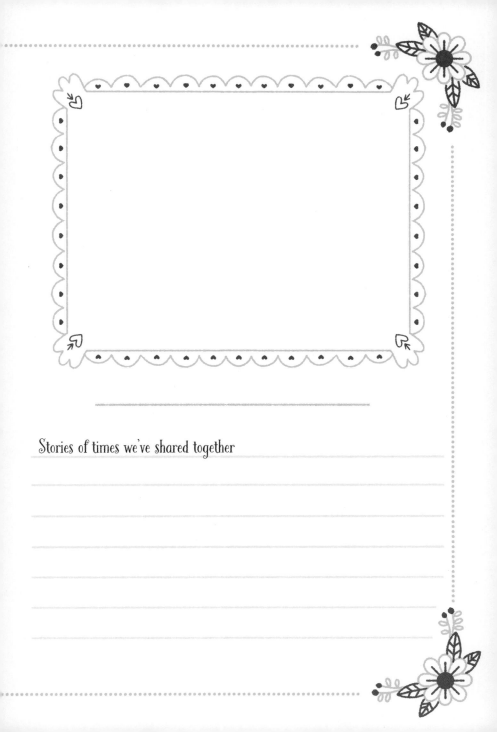

Stories of times we've shared together

_____

_____

_____

_____

_____

_____

The Greatest Influences On My Life

Over the years, various people and places have had a big impact on my life

_____

_____

_____

_____

_____

_____

_____

The decision that changed the course of my life

_____

_____

_____

_____

_____

_____

_____

The most important piece of advice I was ever given

What I am most proud of

My deepest values

Fantasy Page

If I could be any animal I would choose ...

_____

_____

_____

_____

The superpower I would like

_____

_____

_____

The building or place I would most like to live in and why

_____

_____

_____

I would like to be famous for ...

The talent I would like to possess

If I won the lottery ... how I'd spend my millions

Travel

The furthest I've ever travelled

My favourite city

My favourite country

My travelling companions over the years

Holiday photo

_____

A few travel tales
_____
_____
_____
_____
_____
_____
_____
_____

Family Holidays

The first holiday I can remember

Childhood holidays with my family

My favourite place to visit as a child was ...

My most memorable holiday

More Family Holidays

Holidays with my children

The best of times, the worst of times

The funniest moments

My home away from home

How the World Has Changed

When I was a girl the world was a very different place

The biggest changes for me

Things I miss ...

And other things I'm glad have changed

Major Events During My Lifetime

As a child I still remember ...

_____

_____

_____

The most significant events that happened when I was growing up

_____

_____

_____

The most exciting events of my childhood

_____

_____

_____

World Events

Important events I have witnessed as an adult

The event that had the most impact

Exciting news

The most shocking

Regrets

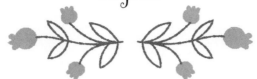

Missed opportunities

My biggest regret

Things I wish I'd done differently

Famous People I've Met

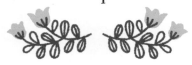

As a teenager, I queued to catch a glimpse of ...

The most famous person I've ever met

The person I would most like to meet and why

When I'm famous I will ...

Hopes

It's never too late ...

_____

_____

_____

_____

_____

_____

_____

_____

_____

_____

_____

_____

_____

_____

_____

My 'to do' wish list

-
-
-
-
-
-
-

Future dreams and plans

_____

_____

_____

_____

_____

_____

_____

_____

_____

_____

The Best Day of My Life

I Almost Forgot

Extra stories I'd like to share

My life story wouldn't be complete without...

First published in Great Britain in 2016 by
Michael O'Mara Books Limited
9 Lion Yard
Tremadoc Road
London SW4 7NQ

A CIP catalogue record for this book is available from the British Library.

Papers used by Michael O'Mara Books Limited are natural,
recyclable products made from wood grown in sustainable
forests. The manufacturing processes conform to the
environmental regulations of the country of origin.

ISBN: 978-1-78243-627-0 in print format

1 2 3 4 5 6 7 8 9 10

www.mombooks.com

Designed by Claire Cater
Cover Illustration by Helen Dardik
Illustrated by Lizzy Doyle

Printed and bound in China